IT'S GREAT TO BE OLD

Happy B-day AL

Laura & Mohamed

2005

IT'S GREAT TO BE OLD
401 REASONS TO STOP LYING ABOUT YOUR AGE!

JIM DALE

ILLUSTRATIONS
BY ED FISCHER

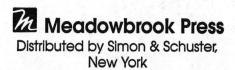

Meadowbrook Press
Distributed by Simon & Schuster,
New York

Library of Congress Cataloging-in-Publication Data

Dale, Jim, 1948-
   It's great to be old: 401 reasons to stop lying about your age! / by Jim Dale.
   p. cm.
   ISBN 0-88166-477-4 (Meadowbrook) ISBN 0-684-02520-5 (Simon & Schuster)
   1. Aged—Miscellanea. 2. Aged—Humor. 3. Old age—Miscellanea. 4. Old age—Humor.
I. Title.

   HQ1061.D265 2004
   305.26'02'07—dc22

                                                                    2004044971

Editorial Director: Christine Zuchora-Walske
Editor: Joseph Gredler
Proofreader: Megan McGinnis
Production Manager: Paul Woods
Graphic Design Manager: Tamara Peterson

© 2004 by Jim Dale

Published by Meadowbrook Press, 5451 Smetana Drive, Minnetonka, Minnesota 55343

www.meadowbrookpress.com

BOOK TRADE DISTRIBUTION by Simon and Schuster, a division of Simon and
Schuster, Inc., 1230 Avenue of the Americas, New York, NY 10020

09 08 07 06 05 04   10 9 8 7 6 5 4 3 2 1

Printed in the United States of America

DEDICATION

To Ellen, with whom I plan
to grow really old.

INTRODUCTION

Welcome to old. Getting old isn't bad. It's good. In fact, it's great. For one thing, you're not young and stupid anymore. For another, young people have to act nice to you. So congratulations. You're old. It took a long time to get here, but it was worth the wait.

YOU'RE SMART.

By now, you know everything. And what you don't know, you can make up.

You aren't neurotic, psychotic, phobic, fixated, or hung up. Who has time for such craziness?

You're "wise." That's the word used for old people.

You don't go to psychics, astrologers, or anyone who predicts the future. If something bad is going to happen, why waste precious time worrying about it?

You don't have an irrational fear of aging.
It's a rational fear.

YOU'RE ESPECIALLY SMARTER THAN YOUNG PEOPLE.

Young people *think* they have all the answers.
You *know* you have all the answers.

Young people stay up late, get up early,
then wonder why they're tired all day. Duh!

 Young people spend a lot of money and are
shocked when they get the bills. You spend
nothing—unless you get a senior discount.

Young people exercise and end up with pulled
muscles, strained backs, and torn ligaments.
You're smart enough to avoid such things.

YOU CAN GIVE ADVICE GENEROUSLY WITHOUT BEING ASKED.

Young people think old people know a lot.
Don't tell them differently.

Young people need your advice. Look at all the
dumb things they do.

Your advice is wise—and free.

You have lots of advice to give. It would
be selfish to keep it all to yourself.
So you give and give and give….

4

YOU CAN GIVE ADVICE ON THINGS YOU KNOW NOTHING ABOUT.

Thermonuclear power. *Be sure to turn it off before you leave.*

Cloning. *Only if we make nice people.*

The Gold Standard. *Invest in shiny things.*

Cold fusion. *Don't lick an icicle. Your tongue could stick to it.*

Complex carbohydrates. *Don't eat anything too complex. Just have three simple meals a day.*

Ozone layer. *What's all the fuss about? It keeps you nice and warm.*

YOUNG PEOPLE GIVE UP
THEIR SEATS FOR YOU.

They feel guilty about sitting in a comfortable seat
while you're standing, especially if you're moaning.

They let you cut in front of them in line,
if you walk with a slight limp.

Some young people stare meanly at others who
won't give up their seats right away.

When a young person offers you a seat, you take it.

They open the door and carry your
packages and let you cross the street
after the traffic light says, "Don't Walk."

YOU DON'T HAVE TO DIET ANYMORE.

You've tried all the diets. They obviously don't work, or you'd already be thin.

Are you suddenly going to be buff after years of being a blob?

Look around. You look like everyone else your age—skinny legs, lumpy thighs, flabby arms, saggy butt.

Dieting isn't for people who like to eat.

YOU HAVE A WHOLE NEW DEFINITION OF "YOUNG."

"Young" is any age two or more years less than yours.

"Old" is any age two or more months more than yours.

"Kids" are adults with children.

"Children" (a.k.a. grandchildren) are the offspring of kids.

"Young" are people who stay up past midnight even though they don't have severe heartburn.

"Young" is anyone who has to think for a minute when asked to name a body part that hurts or has been replaced.

"Young" are people who go to bars on weeknights.

"Young" are people who jog every morning.

"Young" is a state of mind...that has slipped your mind.

IT'S TOO LATE TO GET IN SHAPE.

What are you going to do? Start taking steroids so you can have a wrinkly face and huge pecs? Or a saggy chest and six-pack abs? How will you tell the steroids from all your other medications?

People already know you as someone out of shape. You wouldn't want to confuse them. "Who is that muscular guy who looks like Bob?"

Being out of shape is part of your personality.

Your muscles are too tired to get firm.

Working out takes time. Precious time.

YOU GET DISCOUNTS FOR BEING OLD.

You get into movies for the same price as little kids, except you get to see the R-rated and X-rated shows.

You get deals on dinner if you're willing to eat a little early, which is okay since you probably had breakfast at 5:00 AM and lunch at 10:30 AM.

You get to fly to Florida for less on a plane full of old people who got to fly to Florida for less.

If you don't get a discount, you complain to the store manager. He feels bad because he ignores his parents, so he gives you a discount to ease his guilt.

YOU'RE NOT IN A HURRY.

You don't mind standing in long checkout lines, e̶
if you have only six items. It gives you something t̶
do. Plus, it makes for interesting conversation.

You don't mind being put on hold and listening to
elevator music. Admit it. You sometimes hum along.

You don't complain about bumper-to-bumper
traffic. What's the rush?

You don't choose overnight delivery when you order
things over the phone or Internet. It ruins the fun.
If it takes a long time to arrive, chances are you'll
forget about it. Then it'll be a surprise!

You like to go the mailbox to see if something
came for you. Even on Sunday.

NEED TO LOOK IN
OR ANYMORE.

content with your self-image.
Why ruin everything?

You look better in your memory than
you do in the mirror.

Mirrors lie. And they laugh at you when
you turn your back.

Hey! Who's that person in the mirror wearing
your clothes but looking way heavier, shorter,
dumpier, and wrinklier than you?

14

IN FACT, YOU'RE SO NOT IN A HURRY, YOU HAVE "TIME."

You never press zero to bypass a computer answering system. You're happy to listen to the options and press the buttons.

You slow down *in anticipation* of yellow lights.

You order your fast food just the way you like it...no matter how long it takes.

You read long books. And you don't like it when they end.

You don't mind going through airport security. And you don't mind getting scanned twice.

Sometimes you heat things up on the stove instead of in the microwave, just to be nostalgic.

You always take the scenic route.

YOU DON'T NEED TO RUN. YOU WALK.

Nothing, absolutely nothing, is worth running for.
You've run after things your whole life,
and they've never been worth it.

There's always another bus. That's why
it's called a bus stop.

Even if there's only one elevator,
it has to come down again.

If the traffic light tells you, "Don't walk,"
you don't walk. The stores will still be there
when you get to the other side.

If you walk while it's raining, you get wet. If you run while it's raining, you get wet and out of breath.

Running to catch a cab is crazy. Let the cab come to you. The whole idea is getting a ride.

If you don't make a plane, train, or ferry, you weren't meant to. It was probably going to crash or sink anyway.

If you're late for a movie, you just stroll in. Chances are you missed only the coming attractions or credits. If the movie started already, you ask the person next to you, in a loud voice, "Hey, what happened?"

YOU DON'T HAVE TO GO TO THE CLEANERS AS OFTEN.

You have fewer suits, fewer sport jackets, fewer dresses, fewer skirts, and fewer expensive items that get red wine or marinara sauce spilled on them and have to be taken to the cleaners.

You don't wear a freshly ironed shirt or blouse every day anymore. In fact, you wear nothing but knit pullovers. If you have to get dressier, you wear one with a little guy on a horse or a smiling alligator on the front.

Every day is casual Friday. Also known as messy Friday, wrinkled Friday, and stains-down-the-front Friday.

You don't have anything starched anymore. Starch is for young people who enjoy feeling uncomfortable.

YOU'RE AN EXPERT AT SITTING.
WORLD-CLASS, ACTUALLY.

You sit in front of the TV. It doesn't matter
what's on. You've probably seen it anyway.
Or you've seen it but can't remember it.

You sit at movie theaters. They have big comfortable seats with cup holders for drinks and popcorn
so you can tilt back and talk to the people
around you, even though you practically have
to yell to be heard over the movie.

You sit in chairs (reclining or regular), on sofas (full-size or loveseat), in cars (front seat or back, offering the driver advice wherever you may be), and on futons (whatever a futon is). You have no bias when it comes to sitting devices.

You don't have to be *doing* something all the time...going somewhere, having a meeting, making a deal, on your way out, on your way back. You can just sit...for a long time. Then after a long day of sitting, you can get up and go to bed.

As an expert sitter, you're a great babysitter, too. (See "You can spoil your grandchildren" on page 41.)

IT TAKES LESS...

...to make you full. Half a sandwich, half a banana, half a piece of pie. This explains why there's always half a sandwich, half a banana, and half a piece of pie in your refrigerator.

It takes less to give you gas. Enough said.

It takes less money for you to live. By now, you've bought everything you need, and your stuff never wears out.

It takes less to make you tired. A bad movie, a boring game of cards, a trip to the refrigerator, a glass of wine....

It takes less to get you drunk. Sometimes you just have to be in the same room with someone who's having a drink.

YOU DON'T HAVE TO CLEAN
THE HOUSE AS OFTEN.

There are fewer dishes to wash. And when no
one else is looking, you can wipe off a plate
and stick it back in the cupboard.

There's less laundry. You wear the same
shirt twice if the armpits don't smell.

There's less dusting. You move less now that
you're old. Less movement means less dust.
Less dust means less dusting. It's scientific.

There's no reason to wax the floor.
In fact, there never was.

YOU CAN FALL ASLEEP...ANYWHERE.

At the movies. You can sleep through chase scenes, explosions, bloodcurdling screams, and reenactments of World War II.

On airplanes. You can sleep through crying babies, salespeople on cell phones, overly chipper flight attendants, particularly loud engines, chatty copilots, even turbulence.

At someone's house for dinner. You can fall asleep during the host's fascinating travel story.

In your bathtub. You can fall asleep in the middle of washing your feet.

On the phone with a friend. If he or she takes a long pause, you can doze off and have a dream that you're talking to a friend who's taking a long pause.

After falling asleep several times a day, you can complain that you can't sleep at night.

YOU CAN YELL AT THE TV.

"Don't go in there, detective! The guy behind the door has a gun!"

"You call that a laxative! I tried it and nothing happened! And if there's anything I know, it's laxatives!"

"That's the wrong answer! I know my geography, Alex Trebeck!"

"$40,000 for a car? My first car cost $2,000 and lasted twelve years!"

"Rain? Again? What is this, Noah and the flood?"

"That's not funny! It's dirty, but it's not funny!"

"Don't choose her! She's only after your money!"

"Forget it! I'm not voting for either one of you!"

YOU ACTUALLY WATCH THE WEATHER CHANNEL.

You used to watch the news, but now you watch the weather channel. You have to know what it's going to be outside.

You leave the weather channel on morning, noon, and night. It's your default channel. Your safety net. Your 911 of TV. You need to know what the weather will be like today, what it's like right now, what it'll be like tomorrow, what it'll be like the rest of the week, what it's like up north....

If you ask yourself what difference the weather will make, the answer is none. If it's hot, you'll turn on the air conditioning. If it's cold, you'll wear a coat. If it's wet, you'll drive slower (if that's possible). Your plans will not change. The world will not change. But it's important to know, just in case.

There's a low-pressure system three states away that might come in by the weekend, which would ruin your plans if you had any.

Look, another hurricane. Maybe someday they'll name one after you.

There's an 80% chance of precipitation. A good excuse to call your children and remind them not to go out without umbrellas, even if they live in a different state.

The barometer is falling. That's bad. Or is it good? When it's rising, it's good. Or is it bad? What's a barometer anyway? And what does it have to do with a thunderstorm?

Oh no, it looks like a blizzard is coming. Of course, you're in Florida, so what do you care?

YOU DON'T HAVE TO LIFT HEAVY THINGS ANYMORE.

Young people like to show you how strong
they are. So you let them.

Why risk hurting your back? You let
other people hurt their backs.

You don't carry your suitcase. You roll it.

You don't bend over too much because you know
you could get stuck in that position for years.

Instead of lifting, you tip.

YOU DON'T HAVE MIDLIFE CRISES ANYMORE.

You won't wake up one day and say, "Oh my God! Is this all there is?" You know the answer, "Yep. Enjoy it."

You no longer need to buy a sports car. Driving fast doesn't turn you on. It scares you. You wear your seat belt.

Midlife isn't a crisis anyway. A child who never calls, now that's a crisis.

Even if you had a midlife crisis, you'd keep it to yourself.

Besides, midlife isn't bad. It means you have half your life ahead of you.

IT'S TOO LATE TO GET RICH. SO YOU CAN RELAX ABOUT IT.

Even if you started this minute, how rich could you get?

Why save up for a rainy day when you already have an umbrella and galoshes and a good raincoat?

Hey, these aren't the prime earning years. They're the prime spending years. You're doing your part for the economy.

Why invest for old age when you're already old?

Hey, maybe you can still make a fortune overnight. There's only one way to find out: Go to sleep.

YOU DON'T HAVE TO WORK
YOURSELF TO DEATH.

Work. Now there's a great reason to get up before dawn, come home after dark, and never see your family.

You're through sucking up, kissing butt, and telling your boss his daughter-the-troll is beautiful.

You're not climbing the ladder of success anymore. You're content with the recliner of moderate achievement.

Climbing a ladder is dangerous for people your age.

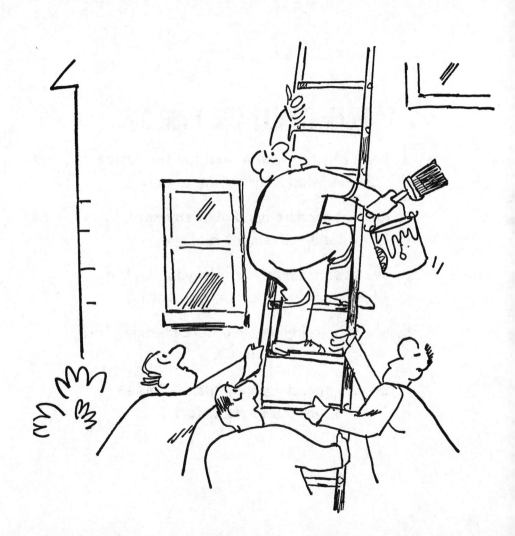

YOU CAN FINALLY USE YOUR IRA.

Way back when, it was a plan for the future.
Guess what? The future is now.

It's not a retirement plan anymore.
It's a retirement reality.

For the first time in your life, you can brag
about how low your tax bracket is.

Remember the rainy day you were planning for?
It's pouring.

You can spend, spend, spend. This is
what you saved it for!

YOU'RE DONE RAISING CHILDREN.

Ha-Ha!

No more diapers, spit-up, potty training, carpools, orthodontists, driver training, curfews, term papers, college applications, or asking, "Have you been drinking/smoking/naked?"

You can tell your kids how to raise their children.

You can tell complete strangers how to raise their children. (See "You can give advice generously without being asked" on page 4.)

You can take credit for your children's successes. *"He's an astronaut today because I used to spin him around until he felt weightless like in outer space."*

Never again do you have to make whirring, zooming noises to get a young child to open the "hangar" for puréed vegetable mush. Until you have grandchildren.

YOU HAVE HOBBIES NOW.

Hobbies are better than work. You don't have to go to hobbies. They're right in your house, in your hobby room.

Instead of dealing with jobs, responsibilities, and errands, you can putter, play, tinker, assemble, construct, collect, and display.

You can count things, knit things, glue things, mount things.

You have boxes of tools, gadgets, and paints made especially for hobbyists.

You can show everybody your hobbies. They'll ooh and aah and ask how you do it, or if you'll make one for them.

You can go to the Garden Show, Boat Show, and RV Show even if you don't have a garden, boat, or dream to drive across the country in a rolling home.

You're very busy.

YOU CAN GET UP EARLY AND NOT WORRY ABOUT GOING TO WORK.

Earlier than the birds.

Earlier than the sun.

Earlier than people in earlier time zones.

Earlier than the president of the United States during times of crisis.

You can get up when it's dark out and go to sleep when it's light.

You can get up so early, it's technically yesterday.

YOU CAN SPOIL YOUR GRANDCHILDREN.

You can buy them things their parents won't buy them, like mesmerizing video games that make annoying *beeps, bleeps,* and *zaps.* You won't be around to listen to the racket.

You can give them candy and snacks their parents won't let them have. *Gooey, sticky, sweet, bad-for-them* snacks that fill them with sugar and chemically alter their brains to make them worship their grandparents.

You can take them places their parents won't take them, like scary movies and amusement parks that make them scream or throw up. Sure, they may wake up with nightmares, but you'll be home sleeping by then.

You can let them stay up late watching videos their parents won't let them watch, and give them more snacks like ice cream, caramel corn, and sugary soft drinks. Boy, will they be hyper when their parents pick them up.

If you don't have grandchildren, you can pester your kids about when they're going to give you some.

YOUR DAY IS HIGHLY EFFICIENT.

You wake up when it's still dark.
In fact, it's still yesterday.

There's no such thing as someone calling
you too early in the morning.

You have breakfast at dawn, lunch at 10:30 AM,
and dinner at 4:00 PM.

You read the morning paper between
breakfast and lunch.

At noon, you take your afternoon nap.

You have your midnight snack at 8:30 PM.

Then you watch the news and call it a night.
(And not the 11:00 news.)

You never watch Jay Leno or David Letterman.
They're on too late.

PEOPLE DON'T BOTHER YOU AFTER 9:00 PM.

Everybody thinks old people fall asleep really early. So people don't call you after 9:00 PM.

You can rent a movie and watch the whole thing without ever having to hit the pause button to answer the phone.

You can read a book and not have to remember where you were when you stopped to answer the phone.

You can take a bath without having to get out and drip across the floor to answer the phone just when it stops ringing.

You can go the toilet without...you get the idea.

If someone calls after 9:00 PM, you can yawn and act foggy when you answer, which will make the person feel guilty. And guilt can be used to get favors.

YOU CAN GO TO FLORIDA A LOT.

You can get a discount on your
airfare just for being old.

When you get there, you can eat early-bird specials.

You can complain about how hot it is to your
friends up north who are digging out of a blizzard.

You can wear loud shorts and knee socks
and T-shirts that say things like,

"I'm not old...compared to a fossil."

"I'm not old. I just have a very full resumé."

*"I'm not old. But I do answer to
the name Fuddy Duddy."*

*"You're only as old as you feel. Come here
and let me feel you."*

"I'm not old. I'm...what was I saying?"

IF YOU GO ENOUGH, YOU CAN BECOME A FLORIDAPHILE.

You can debate Boca versus Naples.

You can play golf all year at every golf course in the state, but still not get any better.

There are over 17,000 delis in Florida. You can eat at all of them.

When you go to restaurants, you can steal rolls from the breadbasket and ask for leftovers from other tables.

You can talk loudly in movie theaters.
It's proper etiquette in Florida.

When your grandchildren visit, you can take
them places their parents won't take them, like
Seaquarium, SeaWorld, Seasickness Park,
and Everglades Overnight Camp.

You can buy your grandchildren overpriced souvenirs
their parents refuse to buy them, like painted coconut
heads, conch shell collections, alligator teeth, stuffed
alligators, and baby pet alligators.

SO WHAT IF A GOOD NIGHT'S SLEEP MEANS GETTING UP ONLY TWICE TO GO TO THE BATHROOM?

When you were young, you could drink all kinds of liquids all day long for an entire weekend and not go to the bathroom until the following Monday.

Now you can drink a thimbleful and go several times a day.

As you get older, your bladder shrinks. Now it's the size of a corn niblet.

The amount of liquid you use to lubricate your toothbrush is enough to wake you up at 1:00 AM, 3:00 AM, and 5:00 AM for bathroom visits.

Do NOT gargle before bedtime.

No matter how many times you go to the bathroom during the day, you'll have to go again in the middle of the night. Multiple times. You'll probably pass your spouse along the way. It's a good time to catch up.

You'll have dreams that you have to go to the bath-room. Don't ignore them. They're based on reality.

Amazingly, when you get up in the morning, the first thing you'll do is go to the bathroom.

YOU'RE NOT A HYPOCHONDRIAC ANYMORE.

Now when you say your joints ache,
it's osteoporosis.

When you say you have gas, it's acid reflux.

When you say your head hurts, it's a migraine.

When you say you have to go to the bathroom, you
have to go to the bathroom!

YOU CAN DRIVE BADLY AND NOT CARE.

You can creep along and pretend
not to hear horns honking.

You can speed and pretend not to
hear horns honking.

You can turn the wrong way down a one-way street
and give that delirious-older-person look.

You can bump into mailboxes, telephone poles, and
shopping carts...and just keep on going.

You can back up without looking. *"That's why I got
a big car. So people would see me coming!"*

You can blame everyone else for your bad driving.
*"If you don't like the way I change lanes,
you should pull off the road!"*

55

YOU GET TO GOSSIP ABOUT PEOPLE'S OPERATIONS.

"What'd they take out? Wow!"

"What'd they put in? Whoa!"

"Was it plastic or metal? Amazing!"

"Where did they do it? Fancy schmancy!"

"Who did it? Fam-ous!"

You can even have dueling operation conversations:

"She had a quadruple!"

"Well, he had a quintuple!"

"Big deal. She got a whole new one!"

YOU'RE AN EXPERT ON PLASTIC SURGERY (A.K.A. "JOBS").

Nose jobs:

- The Full Gentile (a grape with air holes)
- The Modified Melting Pot (the child of an Irish woman and a Jewish man, with her genes dominating)
- The All-American (everyone's nose in Nebraska)

Chin jobs:

- Add-a-Chin
- Reduce-a-Chin (a.k.a. The Anti-Jay Leno)
- The Thanksgiving-Turkey-Excess Neck
- The Chin-Jaw-Neck Combo Deal

Eye jobs:

- Droop Away (lid lift)
- Garbage Day (bag removal)

Boob jobs:

- More More More
- Less Less Less
- Raise the Titanic(s)

Face-Lifts:

- Nip and Tuck (like having your pants taken in after a diet)
- The Age Fighter (forehead up, eyes back, cheeks in and...presto! Your face is ten years younger than your arms, thighs, and butt!)
- The Joan Rivers (skin tightened until a dime will bounce off it; a.k.a. "Oh my God! What have you done?")

YOU'RE NOT YOUNG ANYMORE. THANK GOD!

You don't try to look like teenagers. Teenagers look stupid.

Who wants to have acne, wear baggy jeans, and say *like* all the time?

Who wants to hang out in bars and perfect the art of getting rejected?

It's too late to be a great athlete. What a relief!

You're not obsessed with youth. If you're obsessed with anything, it's regularity.

YOU DON'T HAVE TO KNOW WHAT'S "IN."

Admit it. You have no idea what the newest music is, and you wouldn't like it anyway.

You only like oldies because they're named after you.

Crop tops don't look good over middle-aged bellies. Your jeans already hang off your butt. And torn clothes should be thrown out.

You don't watch reality TV because

1) Kids living in beach houses for free isn't reality.

2) Voting people out of the jungle isn't reality.

3) Having hundreds of slimy bugs crawling on you isn't reality. It's disgusting.

If you want reality, you get a physical.

DANCING FAST OR SLOW IS THE SAME.

How you waltz: Bodies touching; sliding and gliding; no sudden movements; big circles.

How you dance to rock 'n' roll: Bodies not touching; sliding and gliding; occasional jerky gliding; bigger circles.

How you cha-cha: Bodies touching...not touching...touching; sliding and gliding; no sudden movements; big ovals (circles from Central America).

How you bossa nova: See cha-cha.

How you limbo: You don't.

How you dance at a bar mitzvah or bat mitzvah or wedding: Bodies touching (it's a happy event); no sudden movements (all songs are played at exactly the same tempo); sliding and gliding; big circles (in case of the hora, a really big, slightly faster circle). Note: Never let anyone put you on a chair and dance with you up in the air.

YOU NEVER, EVER HAVE TO GO TO DISCOS, CLUBS, OR MOSH PITS.

You don't have to put up with those mirror balls spinning around making you dizzy, or the music blasting, or the people yelling and spilling drinks on you.

You don't have to face a humiliating bouncer who decides who gets in and who doesn't. Admit it. Only the hippest people get in to clubs, not people with the biggest hips.

The mere sound of *mosh pit* is enough to keep you away. "Mosh" is like bad "mush," and a pit is a dark smelly place. Who wants to go to a dark mushy, smelly pit?

The only clubs you're interested in are country clubs where you can wear loud pants and stretchy shirts with animal logos on the front.

YOU DON'T HAVE TO SIT ON THE FLOOR.

Sitting on the floor is for young people. After the age of five, even they don't like it.

Adults who pretend to like sitting on the floor are lying or trying to act like teenagers, who would really prefer sprawling on the sofa.

Who invented the idea that sitting on a cold, hard floor is relaxing or fun? It's cold and hard!

Your back hurts when you sit on the floor.

Your feet dig into your thighs when you sit on the floor.

Your butt hurts when you sit on the floor.

Even in restaurants where you're supposed to sit on the floor, they give you a pillow to sit on and another pillow to lean against the wall, making a...sofa!

YOUR BODY MAKES MUSIC WHEN YOU WALK.

Creak (leg bones, feet, ankles).

Crack (elbows, neck, shoulders).

Honk (nose, throat, sinuses).

Pop (joints).

Click (jaw, teeth, gums).

Thump (heart).

Clank (artificial parts).

Flap (excess flesh).

Flap (more excess flesh).

Plop (body falling into chair after walking).

YOUR PARTIES DON'T DISTURB THE NEIGHBORS.

How noisy can Scrabble be?

How drunk can people get on Ensure?

The only reason police would raid your party would be to look for a drug dealer selling illegal laxatives.

There's no such thing as "blasting" Broadway show tunes.

The loudest moments at your parties occur when someone yells, "Surprise!" and someone else turns up his hearing aid and yells, "What?"

THEY PLAY YOUR MUSIC IN ELEVATORS.

The Beatles performed by the Cleveland
Chamber Society.

The best of Motown by the Mormon
Tabernacle Choir.

Rolling Stones by Big Ten marching bands.

Grateful Dead by barbershop quartets.

Wayne Newton singing Bob Dylan's greatest hits:

"Oh, the times, they are a change-change-changin'..."

"The answer is blowin'—blow-blow-blow—in the wind..."

*"Hey Mr. Tambourine Man—a tam-tam-
tambourine man..."*

SO WHAT IF YOU'RE A LITTLE GASSY?

It's easy to know what you can and cannot eat.
You can't eat anything. But you do anyway.
Hey, what's a little gas?

You used to have a cast-iron stomach and could eat
garlicky, chili-y, red peppery, yellow peppery, Tabasco-y,
horse-radishy foods with sauces that have warning
flames on the bottles...and then sleep like a baby.

Now you use a little mayonnaise and you're up all night
listening to your stomach rumble like Mount Vesuvius.

You enjoy each meal several times. First when you
eat it, then when you burp it up.

Enchiladas, quesadillas, linguini, scampi,
goulash, curry, Hunan, Denny's Grand Slam
Breakfast...all give you gas.

Smelling food gives you gas.

Walking past food gives you gas.

IT'S OKAY TO BE CRANKY.

Young people expect you to be cranky.
You wouldn't want to let them down.

When you're older, crankiness is charming.
Now you're extremely charming.

Crankiness is an art form. A subtle combination
of whining, complaining, and frowning with
a dash of constipation.

Real crankiness takes time and patience. You've
been studying it your whole life. You've earned a
master's degree in crankiness. You're first-team all-
American. You're the MVP. You've won the Olympic
Gold Medal in the crankiness event.

"Who's cranky? And who wants to know?"

YOU GET TO REPEAT YOURSELF.

You get to tell the same stories over and over. Why tell new ones? Your old ones are proven winners.

You can give the same advice over and over. Maybe it'll eventually sink in.

You sometimes forget that you've already said something. Just to be sure, you say it again. And again.

You sometimes say things louder the second time, in case someone didn't hear you.

You repeat yourself. Did we mention that already?

YOU CAN KEEP A SECRET.

Who are you going to tell? Do you know anyone important?

What difference would it make if you told?

You can keep a secret until your dying day. After that, no one will be able to blame you for telling.

You know there's really no such thing as a secret. It's one of those things you learn from being old.

You'll probably forget it anyway.

SO WHAT IF YOU'RE GETTING A FEW WRINKLES?

Wrinkles are a sign of wisdom. You're getting wise over lots of parts of your body.

Your friends are getting wrinkles, too. So you look attractive to each other.

Wrinkles on your face are like road maps of your life. Pretty soon you'll have enough to plan a cross-country trip.

Wrinkles are relative. If you're the oldest relative, you have the most wrinkles.

Just think, if you were born with wrinkles and got smooth skin as you grew older, you'd be rubbing creams on your face to bring back those youthful folds.

YOU CAN SIT IN THE BATHTUB
AS LONG AS YOU WANT.

Go ahead. Take a bubble bath. Soak. Loll. Play with the bubbles. You can't get any wrinklier.

Read a book. Soak. Turn the page. Soak. Turn the page. See the little grooves in your fingers? Don't worry. They were there before you got in.

Wash your hair. Rinse. Condition. Shave. Scrub your back. Dye your hair. Dye it another color. By now you may need to shave again.

Play with a toy boat. Sink the other boats. Make battle noises.

Watch TV. A ball game. In extra innings. The news. A special. A miniseries. A movie. A sequel.

Talk on the phone. Yak. Gossip. Call long distance. Stay on till you get to off-peak time when it costs less.

Stay in while the water drains out. Now count your wrinkles. See? Exactly the same as when you got in. No new wrinkles. Fill up the tub and soak some more.

YOU CAN WATCH MOVIES YOU'VE ALREADY SEEN.

You can't remember seeing them, so it's like watching them for the first time.

Old movies are the best. Somehow you know just when to laugh.

You can guess if the guy is going to get the girl by the time the movie ends.

You aren't scared by surprise endings.

You always guess whodunit.

If you get tired of watching movies you've already seen, you can always read a book you've already read.

SO WHAT IF YOU'RE LOSING YOUR HEARING?

You don't have to listen to anything you don't want to listen to, like advice, or helpful suggestions, or things you disagree with.

You can cut off other cars in traffic and not hear tires screeching and tractor-trailers crashing into guardrails.

When you're in one of those take-a-number lines, you can step up and act like they called your number.

You can turn up the TV really loud. It's no wonder you can't hear the phone, or the doorbell, or advice, or other people begging you to turn down the TV.

YOU HAVE NEW ROLE MODELS.

You used to look up to Mick Jagger because he was young and wild. Now you look up to him because he's a grandfather.

Whoever invented Viagra should have a statue in his or her honor.

How did Strom Thurmond do it (and do it and do it) without Viagra?

Gordie Howe played professional hockey until he was fifty-five.

Sophia Loren and Raquel Welch look good for their age.

How about all those people on Smucker's jars who are over a hundred?

YOU CAN TELL THE SAME JOKES OVER AND OVER.

Old people are supposed to tell old jokes.

"Did I ever tell you the one about the salesman and the sheep farmer?"

They must be good jokes if you've remembered them this long.

New jokes aren't as funny as old jokes.

You get to laugh at your own jokes. You laugh at the punch line even before you get to it.

"Did I ever tell you the one about the salesman and the sheep farmer?"

SO WHAT IF YOU'RE LOSING YOUR EYESIGHT?

You're supporting a whole new industry:
large-print books.

You're amassing a huge collection of reading glasses.
No matter where you go, you always have a pair
handy, if you can remember where you put them.

You can tip low and pretend you read the bill wrong.

You don't see your liver spots so well.

Other people your age look sexy to you.

In fact, the whole world looks like one of those
romantic, out-of-focus movies.

You keep holding things with small type farther and
farther from your eyes. Eventually you'll have to ask
people to take things down the street or across
state lines for you to read them.

YOU CAN FINALLY GET YOUR MONEY'S WORTH FROM YOUR HEALTH INSURANCE.

You paid premiums for years and years and hardly went to the doctor. Now it's payback time.

You can find out what "unlimited visits" really means.

If you think about it, there's something that hurts every day.

Thanks to modern medicine, there's a test for every part of your body. Why not take them all?

The pharmaceutical companies are discovering miracle drugs every day. And you have a prescription copay. Why not try them all?

Look at all the specialists who are "in network." Why not go to them all?

You don't mind sitting in the waiting room. You can relax and read all the issues of *People*, *Time*, and *Field & Stream* from 1998.

So what if you have to fill out a lot of paperwork? What else are you doing today?

IN AN EMERGENCY, NO ONE EXPECTS YOU TO SAVE THE DAY.

Let's be honest. What could you do anyway? Break down the door? Perform the Heimlich maneuver?

You couldn't run for help. You could walk, but not too fast.

You could dial 911 as soon as you found your glasses.

You could try to save the day, but it might create another emergency—saving you.

YOU CAN PRACTICE BLOWING OUT CANDLES.

The older you get, the more you need this skill.

Inhale deeply and see how long you can hold your breath. People under forty need about two seconds per candle. People between forty and sixty need about three seconds. People over sixty need a good minute or two.

Carefully examine the candle layout and figure out the best blowing pattern:
a) Concentric circles; b) Crisscross;
c) Up and down rows (lawnmower-style).

Bring a portable oxygen tank as a backup.

Work on your birthday wish ahead of time.
No one wants to wait while you think of a wish.
People just want cake!

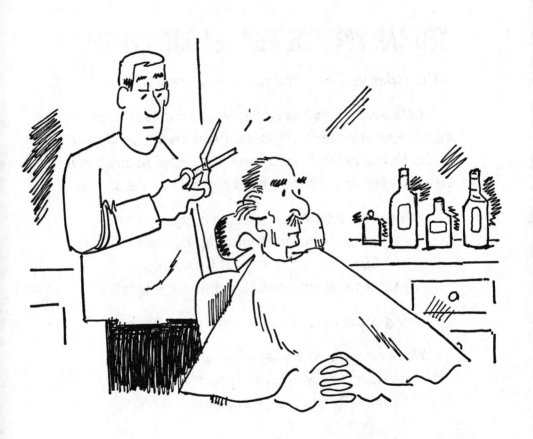

SO WHAT IF YOU'RE LOSING YOUR HAIR?

Less hair means less dandruff, less blow-drying, and less combing over.

Less hair means less bad-hair days.

You're beginning to get that cool, bald-headed look of professional athletes. Except you're older and shorter and don't have a multimillion-dollar endorsement deal from Nike.

For every hair you lose off your head, you gain two more in your ears and nostrils.

SO WHAT IF YOU'RE LOSING YOUR MEMORY?

You can ignore people you never really liked. *"You were my boss? Really? My whole career? Sorry, I can't place the name or face."*

You can skip boring cocktail parties. *"Party? I wasn't invited to a party."*

You can disregard late notices. *"Videos? What videos?"* *"Federal income tax? What federal income tax?"*

You can miss someone's birthday and pretend you forgot. They have to forgive you.

You're losing your memory. Did we cover this already?

Now if you could just remember where you put it.

And where did you leave your glasses? Which pair were you looking for? Reading or distance?

"Where's the portable phone? It was right here next to the remote."

"Who is that guy who looks like me? My brother? What a coincidence."

SO WHAT IF YOU'RE SHRINKING?

You don't have to duck under low doorways any-more. And you have plenty of legroom on airplanes.

Your pants never have to be let out anymore. But they do have to be shortened. And shortened. And shortened.

You can't see over the steering wheel, but you do have an excellent view of the speedometer, which is why you drive very slowly.

Pretty soon you can shop in the children's department.

Pretty soon you can live in a shoebox.

Pretty soon your neck will be a toothpick, your legs will be pencils, your butt will be.... Hey! Where did your butt go?

YOU COULDN'T CARE LESS ABOUT WARRANTIES AND SERVICE PLANS.

What are you going to do with a twenty-year service plan on a toaster oven?

You'd rather outlive your microwave.

You prefer money-back guarantees. If your VCR breaks, you want cash...now.

Nobody wants to get a warranty for a blender in your will. And besides, warranties aren't transferable.

Given a choice between a warranty and a rebate, you take the rebate. It's money. Spend it fast.

YOU CAN RE-GIVE ALL YOUR OLD GIFTS.

Think of the money people have wasted on your gifts over the years. Think of how much you'll save by re-giving those gifts. It's better than an IRA!

Admit it. You've got tons of old gifts stashed in the closet. Ones you've never touched. You'd hate to throw away perfectly good stuff!

Wallets, key chains, novels, luggage tags, desk blotters, pen and pencil sets, clocks, radios, clock radios, photo albums, frames, memo pads, refrigerator magnets, tchotchkes of all shapes and sizes. You have a virtual warehouse of re-givable gifts. If only you had saved the wrapping paper.

How many neckties have you gotten? Hundreds. How many have you liked? Two, maybe three. Neckties don't wear out. The world doesn't need more neckties. By re-giving, you're recycling. It's the responsible thing to do.

Shop at home in the "old-gift cupboard." It's better than the Internet. You don't have to turn on your computer, find a website, or enter your personal information. Just browse and wrap. (Note: Remove old cards before wrapping.)

Warning: Be careful not to give an old gift to the person who gave it to you, unless the person is old, in which case he or she won't remember it anyway.

YOU CAN THREATEN TO TAKE PEOPLE OUT OF YOUR WILL.

When you were young, nobody cared if you said, "Be nice to me or I won't put you in my will." You probably didn't have a dime. Now that you're old, no one knows whether you've got a fortune stashed away.

If a friend or relative is mean to you, give them an icy, thoughtful stare. Then cough and hold your chest while writing the person's name on a little piece of paper. Then fold it and stick it in your pocket.

Close the door to your den and tell your friends and relatives you're thinking about who's been nice to you...and who hasn't.

Leave copies of your estate lawyer's business card lying around the house.

Casually ask relatives questions like, "What would you do if you suddenly had a million dollars?" or, "Should I divide my money equally among family and friends, or leave it to my favorite people?"

Ask someone to do you a really big favor. If the person says, "No," say, "Okay, fine." Then write down the person's name on a piece of paper. (See previous page.) You're keeping score.

YOU HAVE TIME TO FLOSS.

You can now give flossing its due. Your priorities are finally in order.

Time is flossing. Flossing is time.

You enjoy testing waxed versus unwaxed, tape versus cord, nylon versus polymer.

You experiment with a long piece wrapped around your fingers and a short piece pulled back and forth.

You enjoy examining the food particles on your floss: spinach bits, sparerib chunks, steak gristle, orange juice pulp, jujubes, and the ever-challenging popcorn hulls.

Take your time. Get those teeth way in the back.

Floss until you bleed!

YOU DON'T NEED TO BALANCE YOUR CHECKBOOK TO THE PENNY.

You've finally realized it doesn't make any difference.

YOU CAN LIVE DANGEROUSLY.

Go ahead. Smoke a cigarette, you crazy daredevil.

Walk between parked cars. You know you're not supposed to. Your mother told you not to. Laugh in the face of danger! Walk between those bumpers!

Jaywalk. If you've already walked between parked cars and need to raise the thrill level, cut across a busy street! (But do it before rush hour. Look both ways. Listen for oncoming vehicles. And have someone check for cars coming around the corner. Then walk very fast.)

Run with scissors. Another wildly scary act your mother warned you not to do. You could stab your sister. Or the dog. Or bump into a wall and slice your stomach open and bleed all over the shag carpeting. What the heck! Run! Okay, walk fast...but carefully.

Eat sushi. You've heard stories of people going into convulsions from tainted sea creatures wrapped in rice and seaweed. Granted, you've never actually known someone who got sick or died or even got a little tummy ache, but you've heard stories. So pop one in your mouth!

LIFE'S CLICHÉS TURN OUT TO BE TRUE.

"You've got to get up pretty early to fool me." No one gets up early enough to fool you, unless they live in another time zone. And who wants to fool you anyway?

"C'est la vie." a.k.a. *"Shit happens."* It sure does. And there's nothing you can do about it. That's why they call it shit.

"Always look at the bright side." Something to think about after shit happens.

"Live and learn." What choice do you have? Live and get stupid?

"What goes around comes around." But not always. Sometimes people do bad things and nothing happens. Sometimes people do good things and shit happens.

"Today is the first day of the rest of your life." What else would it be?

"*Tomorrow's another day.*" Of course it is. Next week is also another week.

"*Time flies.*" Sums up the previous two clichés. The message? Get moving.

"*Laughter is the best medicine.*" A laxative is good now and then, too.

"*Every cloud has a silver lining.*" The opposite is also true. Every silver lining has a cloud. Don't start thinking things are good or it'll rain on your head.

"*There's a light at the end of the tunnel.*" That's why it's called a tunnel and not a hole.

"*This too shall pass.*" Originally said about gas.

"*Carpe diem.*" Don't carp. Live for today. Seize the opportunity. At any moment you could have a seizure.

YOU CAN STOP AND SMELL THE ROSES.

So go ahead. Stop. Lean over. Smell those roses.
Unless you have allergies.

Sit though entire infomercials. But be careful you
don't get sucked into buying that home hairstyling
center or that flab-away thigh machine.

Watch the leaves turn. If you stare really hard, you can
see them slowly change from green to light green to
greenish yellow to yellowish orange to orangish brown.
The bad news is, you still have to rake them.

You can leave up your window shade and wake
up to light streaming in your window. But watch
out for peeping neighbors.

BY NOW, YOU KNOW JUST ABOUT EVERYTHING THERE IS TO KNOW.

Life is full of questions. You paid attention.
Now you have the answers.

Nobody argues with old people. It's not polite.

Instead of being anxious for it to be tomorrow,
you appreciate today.

You're mature. You better be by now.

You're old. Cool, isn't it?

Also from Meadowbrook Press

✦ *What You Don't Know About Turning 50*
This funny birthday quiz contains outrageous answers to 101 commonly asked questions about turning 50. Illustrated with cartoons by Steve Mark, this book contains everything you always wanted to know about the big five-o.

✦ *What You Don't Know About Retirement*
"**Q**: How can I make sure my friends and family stay in touch? **A**: Move to a vacation spot and live in a place with a pool. **Q**: Why is it dangerous for a retiree to miss the condo-owners association meeting? **A**: They might be elected president." Makes a great gift and provides a funny quiz to make any retirement party more fun.

✦ *Golf's Funniest Anecdotes*
This collection of 185 true and funny anecdotes about famous golfers, including Chi Chi Rodriguez, Lee Travino, Tiger Woods, Arnold Palmer, and Jack Nicklaus, is sure to get any golfer chuckling.

We offer many more titles written to delight, inform, and entertain.
To order books with a credit card or browse our full
selection of titles, visit our website at:

www.meadowbrookpress.com

or call toll-free to place an order, request a free catalog, or ask a question:

1-800-338-2232

Meadowbrook Press • 5451 Smetana Drive • Minnetonka, MN • 55343